[Handwritten inscription:] Zememo... / ...we are a... / ...the world / ...Princes...

Adventures of The Mad Duck

Part 3

My Journey Through 73 Countries

Princess Umul Hatiyya Ibrahim Mahama

Adventures of The Mad Duck © 2017

Princess Umul Hatiyya Ibrahim Mahama

ISBN-13: 978-1977722461

ISBN-10: 1977722466

Edited by Jackie Bates, UK

Cover Design by DESIGNCAN, Ghana

Digital Publishing & Layout by BKC Consulting, Ghana

Printed by Abacus Digital Media, Ghana

Contact the author via

The Mad Duck Company

Accra – Ghana

Email: info@themadduckcompany.com

Website: www.themadduckcompany.com

Tel: + 233 (0) 244355140/ + 233 (0) 575355140

Dedication

To my mother, without whom I wouldn't have come this far. Thank you for all your sacrifices and for giving me the space to take the road less travelled.

Introduction

Have you ever seen an elephant? What about being chased by one? Have you ever slept by the roadside because the vehicle you were riding in broke down? I have experienced all these things and more. I'm a young African woman who likes to do crazy things. Infact, adventure is my middle name. I have even ridden a bicycle from Accra to Tamale in Ghana to raise funds and build a primary school. Do you know how many kilometres that is? 650km. I did that in six days.

As a child, Geography was my favourite subject, and Geography is still a subject I enjoy.

In 2007, I decided to start travelling around the world. I have been to many countries, including Canada, Finland, Djibouti, New Zealand, and Montenegro. Do you know where Montenegro is? Look it up on the world map if you don't know where it is.

I've travelled by train, bus, plane and motorbike. I have seen natural wonders like Victoria Falls in Zimbabwe. Victoria Falls is the largest waterfall in the world. I have also seen buildings that are hundreds of years old.

Travelling around the world, I have experienced the kindness of strangers. Some of them gave me food to eat, a place to sleep, or helped me when I was lost. Some of the stories I will share with you will make you learn, laugh and sometimes make you want to cry.

One thing I know is that this book will inspire you and help you live your dreams. I want to show you that, you can be the business person, artist, scientist, farmer, film maker, writer, adventurer or whatever profession you want to be in the future.

It is possible.

Happy reading.

Table of Contents

Chapter One
Accra to Abidjan by Road

When the year begins, I take a pen, paper, and a map of the world. I then sit down and decide where I want to travel to. This year, the focus was Africa. I came up with the wild idea of travelling from Accra to Guinea Bissau by road. I'd go through Ivory Coast, Liberia, Sierra Leone, Guinea and arrive in Guinea Bissau. I wanted to see these five countries with very little money. Whatever money I had should take me through these countries, but I had to come up with a plan – on how to travel cheaply. Here's my plan:

1. Travel by road
2. Find free places to stay so I don't have to pay
3. Eat local foods

The countries I would be going to are hard to reach, especially by road. Some of these roads get flooded during the rainy season and cannot be used. I knew it would be challenging, but I still wanted to do it, because that's where the action, the learning, the fun, and adventure are. But as the date I was leaving drew closer, I started to worry and even wanted to cancel the trip.

I was worried about being kidnapped, about being sick, about being stuck and not having the internet to contact my family.

Even though I came up with solutions, just in case any of the things I was worried about happened, and I was praying daily and asking God for courage, these fears 'didn't go away'. They persisted, day after day.

Then the D-day arrived.

Ghana – 9th March

I woke up very tired because I'd barely slept. I had to leave the house by 5am to get my bus to Abidjan. I hurriedly took a shower and left the house. My husband Michael took me to the bus station. When the bus moved out of the transport yard, I knew there was no turning back. I was over the moon to be on the road and was no longer afraid or worried. I was in 'adventure' mode – happy, thankful, full of faith, and looking forward to a successful trip.

The STC bus was clean and brand new. The bus also had a USB port so I was able to charge my phone and listen to music. Our first stop was in Takoradi, the capital of the Western Region. We stopped for a 30-minute break to eat and stretch. Takoradi is often referred to as the oil city because of the oil discovered there. One thing that saddened me when I arrived in Takoradi was that the city was not clean.

Because the road to the border in Elubo was tarred, the journey was smooth. I didn't feel I was travelling. When we got to Elubo, at the Ghana side of the border we didn't waste too much time. After about thirty minutes, we crossed the border. On the Ivorian side, things were different. Two men brought benches to the side of the bus, when I saw the benches, I thought they were for us to sit down on. Apparently, they weren't. The benches were for our bags. We all removed our bags from the bus and they were searched individually. That process took about an hour. Then the next processes followed. Our vaccination cards were inspected. After that inspection, I was told I didn't have the right vaccination and had to have an injection. There was a nurse at the border so I went to him to get the injection. It was extremely painful, I even cried. After that, I went to stamp my passport. And then, finally, our bus was allowed to move. We spent about two and a half hours at the border. It was exhausting.

When travelling by road through Africa, you need to come along with a lot of patience. Whenever I'm packing my clothes, I add a big bag of patience. Without patience, I wouldn't survive. Even though travelling by road in some countries is tedious, it's still my favourite means of travel. Road travel is fun, fun, and more fun. You get to see so much more and understand a country better if you travel by road.

Chapter Two
Grilled Tilapia & Atseke

From the border, it was a smooth stretch to Abidjan. Once we arrived, I made my way to my destination in Cocody Angres. I was very hungry and went out to buy food. Even though it was late, the local restaurants were full of people. They were eating *atseke* and *grilled tilapia*, a local Ivorian dish. I also bought *atseke* and *grilled tilapia*. The fish was tasty and extremely spicy, I nearly bit my fingers off because I hadn't eaten such tasty grilled fish before. Even though we have a similar delicacy in Ghana, this one is just different. After eating, I had a shower and went straight to bed.

Abidjan is the largest city in Ivory Coast. It is a coastal city with a population of about 4.5 million residents. The next day, I went into town, to the business district of Le Plateau, which is where many of the banks have their head office. I was meeting my friend, Yves. He knows how much I like food so he treated me to a scrumptious lunch. On the menu was *atseke* and *grilled tilapia*, my favourite Ivorian dish. I ate till I was too full to move.

In Abidjan, I experienced power cuts – also called 'dumsor', just like we have in Accra. I also noticed that the sun rises later and sets about an hour later than it does in Ghana. The next day, I was leaving for the North. I caught a bus to Yamoussoukro, the capital of Ivory Coast. The bus was comfortable, it had air conditioning but it was very noisy because they were showing a loud movie. The road was tarred, so in three hours, I was in Yamoussoukro. Yamoussoukro has a massive church called Basilica of Our Lady of Peace. This grand church was built by the former President Felix Houphouet Boigny. It has a huge green dome on it can seat 18,000 people. I was very happy to see it.

Basilica of Our Lady of Peace – Yamousoukro, Ivory Coast

I left Yamousoukro on a bus which was like a 'trotro', and was packed with passengers and goods. The bus was so full that some passengers were even standing in the aisle. It was also old and rickety. Thankfully I got a good seat; right behind the driver. The bus was so old that I thought it would break down before we got to our destination. I simply prayed and asked God to take us safely. The weather was very hot and because the bus had no air conditioning, inside was steaming hot and smelly. My armpits were smelling too.

On the way, I saw graveyards with graves that looked like houses; they had walls, roofs, gates and padlocks. I was surprised. We passed through so many villages and towns like Bouafle and Daloa. At Duekoue, we had to get off the bus and on to a minibus, which was even more packed with people and goods. I was so tired and hungry now. I couldn't wait to get to my destination; Man. When we finally arrived, I was the happiest woman in the world.

I woke up excited and ready to explore Man. Man is a town in the northern region of Ivory Coast. It has less than 200,000 people. An agricultural town, Man is the largest coffee-producing area in Ivory Coast. Man has a waterfall called La Cascade. After having breakfast of rice and aubergine stew, I went to the waterfall. It wasn't as impressive as it might have been, because it was the dry season, so there wasn't much water. Man is surrounded by mountains and has a very nice view.

In the evening, I bought my favourite meal; *atseke* and *grilled tilapia*. The food was heavenly. This delicious meal is one reason I would return to Ivory Coast.

The next day, I was continuing my journey to a town called Danane. Even though I arrived early at the bus station, we didn't leave till nearly midday. Our bus was full to the brim. The bus was supposed to carry only eighteen passengers, but there were twenty-six of us and plenty of goods. Some passengers were even standing. When we arrived in Danane, there were no vehicles to the border and I had to get a 'taxi moto'; a motorbike taxi.

I didn't really want to ride on a motorbike because I was not comfortable sitting on one. But I had no choice, so I jumped on one and made my way. About fifteen minutes into our journey we reached the first border and

I was asked for money. That was when I realised I wouldn't have enough money for the trip. I had to return to Danane to get money from the ATM. When I tried taking money from it, the machine refused to give me cash. Unfortunately, it was the only ATM in town, and I was stuck.

The only way I could get money was to go back to Man, which was two hours away. I made it back to Man, took money from the ATM and found a vehicle coming to Danane. As usual we were packed in like sardines, this driver was even worse than the previous ones. He wasn't driving with care. He also kept stopping at every village to pick up passengers. The journey back took so long that we didn't arrive until 8:30pm. I was exhausted and very hungry. I bought my favourite food *atseke* and *grilled fish*, had a shower and I went straight to bed.

Chapter Three
My Two Angels

I had a long day ahead of me so I started my journey early. I got on a mo-torbike and left Danane for Gbeunta, the border between Ivory Coast and Liberia. The road was bad; actually, it wasn't a road but a motorbike path. It was a shortcut the motorbike riders used to get to the border. We covered the journey in over an hour. Because we set off early, I was one of the first people at the border and crossed the border immediately it opened.

On a Motorbike from Danane to the Liberian Border

At Logatuo on the Liberian side, things were different. The first immigration officer I met gave me a hard time. I met three different officers and they also gave me a tough time. At the border, I met Francis and Matthew, both Liberians. We got talking and immediately got on well together. We boarded the same vehicle to Monrovia.

The road from Lagatuo to Ganta in Liberia was very bad. About an hour into the journey we had a puncture, and had to wait till the tire was fixed. Luckily, I didn't mind too much because I was having a great time chatting with Matthew and Francis, two angels sent to help me. They had both been to Ghana so we had a lot to talk about. Francis was well-travelled and had visited almost all the countries in West Africa – by road. He gave me lots of tips on how I could move from country to country. We arrived at Ganta for lunch, and Mathew and Francis treated me. I had *GB* and *GB soup*, a traditional Liberian dish, similar to *fufu* and *light soup*.

The landscape and scenery on the way was similar to Ghana. It was very much like travelling from Accra to Kumasi. We went past Gbarnga, Salala and Kakata, and arrived in Monrovia at 6:30pm. When we arrived, Francis made sure that I got to my destination safely. I was extremely grateful for his kindness. In the ten years I have been travelling, people have been so kind to me. In Mali, Switzerland, Canada, or Namibia, people have gone out of their way to help me.

In Monrovia, I was staying with a local, Auntie Rose. I knew I was in the land of 'dumsor' when I arrived. Many houses didn't have electricity. Liberia had suffered with political instability and civil war for some years. However, since 2005, things have improved. Liberia was the first country in Africa to elect a female president. Ellen Johnson Sirleaf, is also the first woman to be elected chair of ECOWAS. Since ECOWAS was formed in 1975, no woman has chaired it. In 2014, Liberia went through another difficult time, there was an outbreak of the Ebola virus. I heard some very sad stories of how people died. Now Liberia is free from Ebola and people are living their normal lives once more; children are going to school, parents are going to work.

I bought a SIM card and was connected to the internet. It was very slow, certainly not as fast as our internet service in Ghana. I needed money and went to the ATM to withdraw it. But I was surprised when I was given US$. In Liberia, both the Liberian dollar and the US dollar are legal tender. You can spend both currencies.

I explored the city. Thomas Boulevard, a street in the city centre, had decent buildings, shops, hotels and houses. President Ellen Johnson Sirleaf, lives off this road. I also visited the old town and Sayon town.

In Monrovia, I saw a number of UN vehicles on the streets. This is because for thirteen years, Liberia had a United Nations Mission. The mission was a large one, about 15,000 military personnel were stationed here. The missions officially ended in 2016, but their presence is still felt.

I spent some time with my cousin Yowome, who had recently moved to Monrovia for work. Yowome was the one who arranged for me to stay with Auntie Rose. I was very grateful because it meant I saved on accommodation.

Liberia is an English speaking country, however the locals speak a kind of English called Liberian Kreyol. I found it difficult to understand. I had to strain my ears to understand a word or two.

For example *'wakabo' means going to town or going out. 'Wata'* *means water. 'Tek tam befo yu vex de ole ma'.* What do you think this sentence means? In plain english this means *'be careful you don't get mother angry'.* (From Craking the Code: The Confused Travellers guide to Liberian English)

Monrovia has a few four-star hotels and supermarkets catering for the expatriates and wealthy few. I was invited to one of these posh places and got to experience the unusual side of Monrovia. Waheed, a family friend, was in town for business and invited me for dinner. Being in Monrovia made me appreciate Accra much more. Accra is definitely not Singapore, but it's miles ahead of Monrovia. I really admired the citizens of Liberia who are doing everything they can to make ends meet.

Chapter Four

Crawling to Sierra Leone

From Monrovia, I headed for Freetown. I knew the journey was not going to be easy because it was a very long way and the roads were in a terrible condition. My first leg was a bush taxi ride to Bo Waterside, a town on the border between Liberia and Sierra Leone. Then I crossed into Sierra Leone. From the border town, Gendema, I boarded a vehicle for Bo, a city in the southern part of Sierra Leone. Bo Waterside and Bo are two different towns.

Sierra Leone was my sixty-fifth country. I couldn't believe I had come this far. Just thinking back to when I started this journey ten years ago, brought tears to my eyes. Ten years ago, all I had was a dream, a plan, and plenty of determination.

All the guide books I used warned me about the roads, Francis also told me how difficult this stretch will be. I knew my patience and endurance would be severely tested. The Toyota Land Cruiser I took, looked like it would break down any minute. It filled up pretty quickly and I was squeezed into the back seat with three other passengers. Before the journey begun, my bum started aching. The road from Gendema to Zimmi was possibly one of the worst roads I have travelled on. It's a 'road' with valleys, hills, and ponds. It took us three and a half hours to cover a very small stretch. The driver was going so slowly that If I'd walked, I could have moved much quicker than the vehicle. The bumps on the road were something else. I screamed and ouched for those three and a half hours because of the severe bumping. From Zimmi, the roads were still terrible but slightly better than the previous road. When we got to Moa, we boarded a manual ferry crossing over the Moa river into Potoru. It was the first time I had ever used a manual ferry. Though it was a small river, it took us seven-minutes to cross it. I guess if we were on a motorised ferry we would have crossed in less than two minutes.

Crossing a manual ferry – Potoru, Sierra Leone

From Poturo, we pushed on to a town called Bandajuma. We finally arrived in Bo at 6pm. Not only was I mashed and tired, I was desperate for a shower. Because of the dirt roads, I was so dirty and smelly. A fellow passenger, Samuel Kamara, a businessman who lived in Bo, dropped me off at the station to continue my journey to Freetown. Samuel was a very funny and wise guy. He made me laugh throughout the journey. Even though I was so tired,

I still had about four more hours to be on the road before I arrived at my final destination.

Thankfully the last leg of the journey, from Bo to Freetown, was not as tiring. The taxi I boarded was fairly new and carried the correct number of passengers. I was the only foreigner on board, the other passengers were all locals. Because I was a foreigner they looked out for me and wanted to help me. I was thankful for their kindness.

Bo, often referred to as Bo Town, is in the Southern Province. It is Sierra Leone's second largest city. The road from Bo to Freetown was a first-class road. I was happy to finally be away from those dirt roads. When we arrived at Freetown at 10pm, I was very, very happy and heaved a huge sigh of relief. This journey had taken me over fourteen hours to cover. Francis, the angel I met on my way to Liberia, had arranged a place for me to stay. I was staying with Pastor Jeremiah and his family. I finally retired to bed around 11:30pm. What an incredibly long day!

Chapter Five

Concrete City

Freetown, a city of about 2 million people, was in perpetual darkness. Electricity is not widely available. Individuals and businesses generally use a generator. According to a few people I spoke to, Freetown was growing and developing. Sierra Leone is where it is today because for eleven years, it went through a civil war. Millions of people left the country and thousands died. Thank God, the war has now ended. Sierra Leone is rich in diamonds but unfortunately, its people are poor.

Sierra Leone was also badly affected during the Ebola crisis of 2014. Since it was declared Ebola free, Sierra Leone is making steady progress.

On the streets of Freetown, I was happy to see the GN bank, the Ghanaian bank owned by Groupe Ndoum, I felt very proud. UBA and Ecobank were also operating here.

Though the official language of Sierra Leone is English, the locals speak a kind of English called Krio. Just like in Liberia, I had to listen hard before I could pick up what was being said. For example, *'aw di bodi' means how are you? 'Porsin de yu we sabi tok inglish' means Is there someone here who speaks English?*

From Freetown, I pushed on to the border. I was going to Guinea. Auntie Joy, Pastor Jerimiah's wife, dropped me off at the station. The road was in a very good condition, which was a relief. It was tarred, so the ride was enjoyable.

In Sierra Leone, I found many similarities with Ghana and the countries I had just come through. The towns, villages, way of life were not different at all. Even the style of buildings. The town of Port Loko in the Northern Province looked just like a town in Ghana.

When we crossed the border into Pamelap in Guinea, I boarded another vehicle to Conakry. This taxi was a motorcaravan and had bags of corn and gallons of palm oil strapped on top. The roads into Conakry were terrible, also I had a hard time with the immigration officials because, they kept asking for bribes.

We arrived in Conakry after 6pm. Motorbikes were zig-zagging on the roads and drivers were not following road traffic regulations. It was rush hour, and there was so much traffic on the roads.

Guinea, often referred to as Guinea-Conakry to differentiate it from all the other Guineas; Guinea Bissau, and Equatorial Guinea, is a country in the Gulf of Guinea. Bordering six countries, Guinea has a population of about 11 million people. It's a French-speaking country, and Islam is the main religion. Rich in minerals, Guinea is the second largest producer of bauxite. Conakry is the capital. I call Conakry the concrete city – because that's all I saw. Concrete everywhere.

I stayed in Conakry for only one night because there wasn't much to see. I decided to go to the Fouta Djallon region instead. I learnt about the Fouta Djallon region in my Geography class over twenty years ago. The area has many mountains, and the rainfall is usually high, so it's very green.

The following day, I woke up and realised I was suffering from diarrhea. I had eaten a dish the night before, which didn't sit well in my stomach. I was on the balcony of the hostel when suddenly I felt a sharp movement in my stomach, but before I could walk to the toilet, something terrible happened, I 'pooed' on myself. I couldn't believe such a thing could happen to a grown woman like me. I was glad there was no one around. I quickly went for toilet roll and cleaned the mess I had made. I then took some ORS and hoped nothing similar would happen on my journey.

Where I was staying in Conakry, Miniere, looked very much like some parts of Accra. There was even an MTN shop there. When I started my journey, I realised that MTN operates in Ivory Coast, Liberia, Sierra Leone and now Guinea. MTN is truly a big company.

At the bus station, I boarded a taxi heading for Mamou, the second largest city in Guinea. The taxi/bus station was similar to what we have Kaneshie, or Nima in Accra. There were no urinals in sight, people urinated anywhere, so the place stank.

At the station, I bought some delicious jollof rice, jollof rice is a dish eaten in West Africa. Surprisingly, this jollof rice was 'white' not 'red' like the jollof rice I am used to eating. It was equally tasty even though it was a different colour.

All the other passengers on board were Fulas; they are the largest ethnic group in Guinea, followed by the Mandinkas.

I had a hard time with the immigration officers at the various checkpoints. The road to Mamou is very busy, crammed with trucks, taxis and buses. As well as being busy, it was terrible, full of potholes – too many to count. The road also had very sharp curves, so even though I was sleepy, I couldn't afford to close my eyes. The journey took us nearly ten hours, when we arrived in Mamou at midnight. I was so overjoyed. A lady I'd met in the taxi, Rukiyatu, asked me to spend the night in her house. I was thankful for her kindness. When we arrived in her house, I took a quick shower and lay down to sleep. I was very tired.

The next day, I met Rukiyatu's family; her daughter who is about eight years old, her mother, aunties, and sisters. They were warm and very happy to see me. I thanked them for their kindness and left. From Mamou I was going to Dalaba, a town further north.

I arrived in Dalaba on a busy market day, and stayed in a hotel run by Catholic nuns. My room was clean and had running water. I went to the market and bought some vegetables and also walked around. Dalaba has the highest altitude in Guinea and is surrounded by mountains.

Chapter Six

Stuck in the Middle of Nowhere

I left Dalaba for Labe. In Labe, I bought some local food, and headed for the station to board another vehicle to Koundara which is further north of Guinea.

The vehicle I boarded, loaded the carrier with goods until it was overflowing. Even though the driver had already loaded so many goods on top of the vehicle, he stopped to pick up another passenger and a motorbike. Yes, I said a motorbike. Can you imagine so many goods on top of the vehicle and now a motorbike? I became angry at this stage and asked him to take me back to the station so I could board another vehicle but he convinced me that his vehicle was safe, and I foolishly believed him.

The over loaded vehicle – Labe, Guinea

This driver drove recklessly. He was speeding when he should be slowing down and navigating sharp turns without even blowing his horn to alert an on-coming vehicle. I was furious. When we started, the road was fine, then we hit a terrible dirt part. We crawled on that dirt road for nearly two hours. Our vehicle even developed a fault and we stopped to fix it. In the middle of nowhere, he stopped, and that's when he realised the vehicle was overheating. Once he tried to restart it, the unthinkable happened; the vehicle refused to start. This was around 7pm.

The driver called for a mechanic, who promised to come and fix it. But the mechanic was far away and I knew he won't arrive until the next morning. I knew we'd be sleeping by the roadside. The locals must have been used to this happening, because they immediately brought out their mats and stretched them by the roadside, ready to sleep.

I just remained in the vehicle. By 10pm I was exhausted and beside myself. Other vehicles using the road kept stopping to ask if they could help us.

They couldn't help, though, because their vehicles were all already carrying more passengers than necessary. One caravan that stopped was carrying sixteen passengers. Four people even sat on top of the goods on the roof, two were in the boot and the rest in the vehicle. For a vehicle that was supposed to carry eight passengers, there certainly wasn't room for anyone else.

At 11pm I dozed off to sleep, but I kept waking up because the caravans kept stopping to find out what was wrong with our vehicle. I finally woke up at 3am. The sky was brightly lit, and the stars were shinning. The only noise I could hear was birds chirping and cows mooing. At 4am the mechanic arrived with his tools then the work began. The diarrhea I suffered a few days earlier, seemed to have worsened in the wee hours of the morning. In forty minutes, I visited the bush four times. I took ORS – medicine to stop the diarrhea. Then I felt better.

At 6:30am the sun rose, it was bright yellow and was moving slowly over the trees and mountains. I couldn't believe the beauty around me. Even though I was worried and wondering how I would get to my destination, I took time to admire and enjoy the beauty. I hadn't spoken to my family in a few days so I called them. Speaking to them made me very happy. After that call, I had some energy and continued to think about my next steps.

I made up my mind to find another means of transport to Koundara. This was because the mechanic wasn't making any progress. The car still hadn't started. A motorbike rider came by and spoke to me, and I told him what had happened. He couldn't give me a lift because he was already carrying his wife and a baby. They were riding all the way to Gambia, which was quite a distance away. When I saw him, I was encouraged and realised I could get to my next point on a motorbike, even though I don't like them and would prefer not to ride on one. But sometimes you have no choice!

Around 8am I saw another motorbike rider. I stopped him and asked if he could take me to Koundara which was about four hours away. He said yes. I was very happy he agreed to take me. This was also an opportunity for him to make more money. We settled on a price.

The driver refused to give me some of my money back, even though he'd clearly failed to get me to my destination. I just left him, put my luggage on the motorbike, and we left. I had a long journey ahead of me and I couldn't afford to waste time or to be angry. The roads were in excellent condition so Mahamadou could go fast when he got the chance. I kept squeezing his shoulder, saying, 'Monsieur, vit vit.' Mahamadou, a Fulani, spoke some French, so communicating with him was fairly easy.

After almost two hours, we arrived in a small town, the first I'd seen since we left Labe. I got off to stretch as my bum was aching. After ten minutes, we pushed on. The weather was extremely hot. It reminded me so much of Tamale in the Northern Region of Ghana. The houses in the villages we went past looked exactly the same – round huts with thatched roofs; cattle and goats roaming around the compound. This area didn't have a lot of people, it was sparsely populated.

Chapter Seven

Finally in Koundara

At 11am we zoomed into Koundara. I was delighted. I washed my dirty hands, bought some food, changed money and I was ready to move on. I thanked Mahamadou very much, I had no doubt that he was sent by God to help me reach my destination. I said goodbye and I boarded a taxi to my next destination; Sareboido.

The two-hour journey from Koundara to Sareboido was quick. Even though the roads were untarred, they were graded and didn't have potholes. From Sareboido to the border town of Buruntuma, I had to get a 'taxi motor' because vehicles didn't ply that route. Even though I was extremely tired and wanted to rest, I couldn't. I bought water to quench my thirst and was on the move again. After about twenty minutes, we had a puncture and had to stop. I had to carry my luggage while the bike rider pushed the bike. The weather was unbearable at this stage. I was angry, tired, and fed up but I had no choice. Thankfully I didn't have to walk for too long; another motorbike came by and carried me. I squeezed onto the bike because he was already carrying one passenger and some goods. So now, we were three adults and three bags.

At Kandika, the last village before the border, I got my passport stamped and headed for Buruntuma. Finally, around 2pm, the miracle happened. I was in Guinea Bissau. My relief when I crossed the border was unimaginable. To think that I had endured so much to get here brought tears to my eyes – tears of joy of course. I couldn't believe it had taken me three days. If the roads were good I could have been here in twelve hours.

I was exhausted, and very dirty, but I was happy. I couldn't celebrate yet because I was still a long way from Bissau, my final destination. Because the roads are so bad, I knew I could be travelling for hours on end, perhaps even a full day.

I boarded a vehicle from Buruntuma to my next destination; Gabu. The vehicle, an old rickety bus, looked like it had been on the road before I was born. It was crawling. And finally broke down. Just then, another vehicle came by and I quickly jumped into it, paying another fare. At this point I was so desperate to get to Bissau I would do anything possible to get there. Thankfully that vehicle, also very old, took us slowly until we got to Gabu.

From Gabu, I boarded a taxi to Bissau. This taxi charged a reasonable fare and didn't squeeze us in like sardines. Once the journey begun, I dropped off to sleep, I was too tired to stay awake. Even though I was asleep, I could feel the vehicle jumping up and down because of the bad roads. At 10pm we arrived in Bissau. I could now celebrate. At last!

I noticed that some parts of the city had lights and others were in total darkness. 'Dumsor' was alive and well in Bissau too. I found some food to eat and then found a hotel. I took a shower and washed away all the dirt I had gathered in the last two days. It was such a relief to have finally arrived.

Chapter Eight

Celebration at Last

Bissau was my final destination. From there I was flying back to Accra. I was happy to say goodbye to the bad roads. If I had returned to Accra by road, I would have needed to rest for maybe a month. The air ticket I was using was bought for me by my family and friends. I made an announcement to them that I needed a ticket back and a number of people responded to my request and sent me the money to buy it. I was super grateful to all those who showed me such kindness.

I woke up bright and early, had my bath and headed for Osvaldo Vieira International airport, the main airport in Bissau. There were a few modern buildings on the way to the airport; the Supreme Court and some other government ministries.

Even though I was going to Accra, I had to fly further away, to Casablanca in Morocco, before I could get to a flight home. In Casablanca, I spent time writing and thinking about all that I had seen and endured in the last few weeks.

When I started this trip, I knew it was going to be tough. But like all things I didn't know it would be this tough. Before I left Accra, I made up my mind to face whatever challenges came my way. With my experience of traveling, I knew I had to enjoy every moment of it. Moments that would enrich and change me. Even though I faced difficult situations, I knew I couldn't be stressed or afraid. I had to trust God to help me in every situation, and that's exactly what happened. The strangers who helped me along the way were all God sent. God truly watched over me.

The seven-and-a-half-hour flight from Bissau through Monrovia was smooth. In the early hours of the morning, we landed in Accra. Now I could really celebrate.

At the airport, I broke down and cried – tears of joy. From the airport, with its modern buildings, Accra looked nice, definitely much nicer than the cities I had just visited. The children were over the moon to see me. I had conquered sixty-seven countries, and so many more to go! I like to drink tea and so I celebrated my success with a lovely cup of tea. It was good to be back home. Back into a clean bed, into a world I am familiar with.

The next few days, I would catch up with the children and rest. But I knew after a few weeks of being home, I'd start thinking about where I want to go next. I agree with Helen Keller, the American author and activist who put it this way 'Life is either a daring adventure or nothing'. Travel is my life, travel is the air I breathe, travel is who I am.

Chapter Nine

Freezing in Zambia

After my trip to Guinea Bissau, I was keen to reach the seventy countries mark. I couldn't wait till my usual travel time in September. I wanted to see the gigantic Victoria Falls in Zimbabwe, and also visit Ethiopia in East Africa.

On this trip, I would be flying a Boeing 787 Dreamliner for the first time, on Ethiopian Airlines. Dreamliners are huge. As soon as I boarded, I noticed that the windows were larger than the normal size. When service began, I ate my food in less than ten minutes, and I wasn't satisfied. I asked the air stewardess for another portion and thankfully she gave me another.

After being in the air for five-and-a-half hours, we landed at Bole International airport in Addis Ababa. My next flight to Lusaka was on the tarmac, ready for us to board. This plane was much smaller, a Boeing 777-200. In less than four hours we arrived in Lusaka.

When we arrived, I was disappointed to see how old Kenneth Kaunda International Airport looked. Later, I realised that a newer and nicer terminal was being built. It cost millions of US dollars. The new terminal is more befitting copper-rich Zambia and is expected to be completed in 2019. Instead of heading straight to a hotel, I decided to wait in the airport to save money. But I was in the lobby and it was freezing cold, it was winter in Zambia. I wore a jacket and wrapped myself in a blanket and also had a hot cup of tea but, I was still very cold. I couldn't wait for the day to break. In the morning, I got in a taxi to the Inter City Bus terminal in downtown Lusaka.

Inter City Bus terminal was like any long-distance bus terminal in Dakar or Nairobi. There were porters rushing to carry my luggage. I bought a ticket for one of the buses; King Lion bus. While we were waiting for the coach to be full, traders kept coming onto the bus to sell their products. People were selling bread, drinks, mobile phone chargers, and even jackets. I counted not less than fifty of those traders. Possibly this is because the people of Lusaka are business-minded.

Once the bus was full, we were off. Just when we got out of the station, the President of Zambia was passing by. We had to wait for him to pass before we continued. Some of the porters at the bus station were excited to see him and waved at him.

Because I was exhausted from the travel and the freezing airport, once we got out of Lusaka I slept. It was a long way to Harare.

Chapter Ten

Where is the Cash?

I was woken up at Chirundu, the border between Zambia and Zimbabwe. Because of all the experience I've had crossing African borders especially, I always come prepared with lots of time and patience – I bring them in my luggage. We stamped our passports, brought out all our luggage from the coach, then waited for our turn to be searched, then waited again for the coach to be searched, then waited some more for only God knows what.

After two-and-a-half hours, all the checks were completed and we boarded and moved on. This border crossing reminded me of the border between Ghana and Ivory Coast. At a town called Karoi, we stopped for a brief break then continued. In the villages after Karoi, I saw compound houses, very much like the compound houses in the northern part of Ghana or the northern part of Guinea; round huts with thatched roofs. The villages were also sparsely populated. The roads were not the best. Our driver had to keep swerving the potholes in them.

Around 8pm, we arrived in Harare, the capital of Zimbabwe. At Road Port terminal, I found a taxi, bought some food and we headed for Greendale, the area where I was staying. On our way, I wanted to take money from an ATM. That's when I realised Zimbabwe was going through a cash crisis. There was no money in the ATM. Thankfully I had money to pay the driver.

I was in Harare to attend a friend's wedding. My friend Samuel, a Ghanaian, was getting married to Rose, a Zimbabwean. Harare was a family affair so I felt very much at home. My dear friends Daniel and Maame Adoma and their children Jeremy, Alison and Adelise, were here. (It was Daniel and Maame who sent me money when my purse was stolen in Madrid, Spain some years back).

The next day, I was out looking for cash, but still couldn't find any.

Daniel and I visited an abattoir to buy meat. I was impressed with this abattoir. It was clean, well-equipped, and had different freezing rooms. Many years ago, Zimbabwe used to export beef to other parts of the world. In Harare, I noticed how nicely woven their thatch houses are. The roofs are so attractive.

From the abattoir, we went to Mbare Musika – a market in town – to buy some foodstuff.

Zimbabwe is an English-speaking country. I was happy to see that majority of people can speak English. Taxi drivers, bus conductors, market women, petty traders – everyone spoke English. I was impressed.

The wedding between Sam and Rose was beautiful. I was one of the photographers on the day and took tons and tons of photos. I got to see the fun-loving nature of Zimbabweans. The guests shared jokes and danced their hearts out.

On the Sunday, I visit a local church, Jabula New Life Covenant Church, pastored by Bishop Tudor and Pastor Chichi Bismark.

Some parts of Harare are beautiful; the flowers, wide streets, neat lawns and unique trees. Zimbabwe, once called the 'jewel of Africa' by Tanzanian president Julius Nyerere, was advanced in farming, manufacturing, and banking. Zimbabwe was a bright light in Africa. However, things changed in the late 1990s when land was taken from white farmers and given to black owners.

When this happened, the white farmers left Zimbabwe. They went to other countries like South Africa and Namibia. Many people became unemployed and couldn't feed their families. So they also left, moving to neighbouring South Africa, Botswana, the United Kingdom and other parts of the world.

Because Zimbabwe was importing much more than it exported, it literally ran out of money to pay for its goods and services. Zimbabwe's currency became worthless and could not be spent. They now started spending other people's currency; US Dollars, South African Rand, Euros, and then bond notes. In Harare, I found almost everything expensive. Fruits and vegetables were the only items I found cheap.

After four days, I still couldn't find an ATM with money, so I had to get my sister Antonia to send me money. When I picked up the money from the Western Union store, I was a happy woman again.

From Harare, I got on a bus for Chimoio in Mozambique. On our way, we went through towns like Marondera, Rusape, and Mutare, arriving at the border before 7am. Crossing the Zimbabwean side of the border was simple, it certainly wasn't as tiring as crossing from Zambia into Zimbabwe. We all got down from the vehicle and had our passports stamped and were done in thirty minutes. Our bags were not brought out of the vehicle and searched – something that could take hours.

Chapter Eleven

Giant King Prawns

I needed a visa to enter Mozambique, but I didn't have one, and planned to get the visa at the border. I started the process but was delayed so much so that the bus I was on left me behind. The conductor brought my luggage from the bus and refunded some money to me to board another vehicle. I was really upset that things turned out this way. I was patient and continued to wait until I was called in for an interview. After the interview, I was given the visa and was free to go.

I smiled and thanked them for letting me into Mozambique. When I stepped out of that immigration zone, I began to dance. I was so happy, because Mozambique was my seventieth country. I couldn't believe how far my dream had brought me.

Trying to get a minibus to Chimoio was a struggle. There were so many people looking for a bus. I finally found one, and was squeezed in it till I felt I couldn't breathe. Even though I was uncomfortable in the vehicle, I knew immediately we began the journey that·I was in for a good ride. The ride to Chimoio was enjoyable because there was so much to look at. I saw trees in various shades of green, mountains and lakes. After a town called Manica, I was surprised to see villages similar to villages in Northern Ghana; round huts, thatched roofs – but not as dry as Northern Ghana. Because the area receives a high amount of rainfall, the vegetation is green and lush. Seeing how similar the area was to the Northern Region of Ghana and the Northern Region of Guinea, I realised that Africans are more similar than different. Though we speak different languages, and have different cultures, we are all one people.

I found a cheap hostel not far from the bus station and lodged there. Chimoio, in central Mozambique, is the country's fifth-largest city. It is a bustling town with a population of over 230,000 people. Chimoio has banks, restaurants, markets and all that I needed to make my stay here comfortable. When I saw a Barclays bank, I quickly rushed to the ATM and took money. It was very different from Zimbabwe and such a relief to know I wouldn't have any problems with money.

In Mozambique things were much cheaper than in Zimbabwe. Food, accommodation, and telecommunication. Interestingly, telecommunication was even much cheaper than in Ghana. The internet was not only cheap but worked very well. I was on cloud nine. Since Mozambique was my seventieth country, I decided to have a little celebration to mark this important milestone. I went to a local restaurant and had a scrumptious dish of *chima*, (a starchy dish made with corn), with beef sauce and kove. *Chima* wasn't new to me because, I had eaten it many times. It is a staple dish eaten in East and Southern African. In South Africa and Namibia, it is *pap*, in Malawi it is *nsima*, in Kenya *ugali*, in Zimbabwe *sadza* and Rwanda it is *ubugali*. Different names but the same meal.

In the hostel I was staying, I met an interesting guy called Rick. Rick is also referred to as the Cycling Dutchman because, he's travelling around the world on a bicycle. Nearly two years before, he'd started his journey from The Netherlands and was now in Mozambique. Since his journey began, Rick had cycled to over sixty countries.

The Cycling Dutchman – Chimoio, Mozambique

Rick shared so many stories with me about the people he'd met. He told me how he carried children to school on his bicycle, was given food to eat by strangers, and places to sleep for free. When he talked about all the people who had been kind to him, I remembered all those who had been kind to me too. My mind went back to the generosity of Rukiyatu when I was in Mamou, Guinea; and the Eastern European guy who gave me a train ticket when I was nearly stuck in Zurich, Switzerland. Travelling has always revealed the kindness of people to me.

Because Rick cycled through remote villages, some people in some of the villages he cycled through were surprised he came all the way from The Netherlands on a bicycle. Rick had travelled to so many countries. About

120 countries in total. Talking about Rick, you might think he is a very old man because he has achieved so much in his life. But no. Rick is not an old man at all, he is only twenty-two. Rick reminded me again that you are never too young to dream and never too young to achieve your dreams.

I hope one day, I will meet Africans as young as Rick travelling around the world. I even hope I will meet them walking, running, riding a motorbike, sailing or riding in a wheelbarrow.

I woke up in a panic when I realized I might miss my bus to Maputo. I jumped out of bed, got the security to find me a taxi, stuffed my clothes in my rucksack and ran out.

The station was only five minutes away, however by the time we got there, I was told the bus had left about two minutes before. I asked the driver of the taxi to head in the direction the bus went as fast as he could. After about a minute driving at top speed, we caught up with the bus. It was a relief. If I'd missed that bus I would have been in big trouble. I'd bought a ticket the day before and had also left my suitcase on the bus. I would have struggled to get my luggage back. Every day, only one bus goes to Maputo, meaning I would have had to wait another day and I didn't have time for that.

When I was finally on the bus, it felt like I had won the jackpot. I was extremely thankful.

Maputo was 1,135km away and the bus ride was supposed to take fourteen hours. I had an open mind because it could take much, much longer. One thing I prayed against was our vehicle breaking down. If that happened, we would be in hot water.

From Chimoio, we passed through towns such as Inchope, Save (pronounced Savey), Pambarra and Massinga. Around 12 noon, I started to get very hungry and couldn't wait to eat. At 3:30pm we arrived at Maxixe (pronounced Mashishi), where we had a very short break. I bought food and had to eat it on the bus. Further from Maxixi, the tire needed changing, and the driver stopped to do that. I was grateful it was only the tire and not a major fault. After thirty minutes, we were on our way. When we got to Xai-Xai (pronounced Shai-Shai) I knew we were getting closer. At half past midnight, we arrived in Maputo. The journey had taken nineteen-and-a-half hours,and I was extremely tired by the time we arrived. I couldn't complain because I'd be travelling back by the same route.

I was excited to finally be in Maputo, where I would be staying with Musah, his wife Anda and their children Saha, Tahama and Baba. I went straight to their house, and after taking a bath and eating, I went to bed. I was exhausted from all the travels, so for the first two days, I stayed indoors and rested.

Mozambique was colonised by the Portuguese, so it is a Portuguese-speaking country.

Olá means Hello

Como esta – How are you doing?

Três – Three

Quatro – Four

Cinco – Five

Quarenta e cinco – Forty- five

Mozambique is a large country. It's almost four times the size of Ghana (about the size of Turkey) making it the thirty-fifth-largest country in the world. It is bordered by six countries, and is rich in natural gas. The total population of Mozambique is over 24 million people.

In Maputo, I noticed that the streets were named so it was easy to navigate. I used Google map to find my way about. On my first night, Musah and Anda took me out to dinner to a posh restaurant called Zambi, on the Maputo Waterfront. I ate giant king prawns; the meal was scrumptious. I also enjoyed a desert called petit gateau. This moist and delicious cake is filled with chocolate, when you take a bite, the chocolate oozes out. This chocolate dessert is one of the most delicious deserts I have ever eaten. That night was special because I really ate.

Maputo also has some Indian roots – Indians moved here many, many years ago. It has a beautiful coastline, palm trees lined along the roads and pretty, Mediterranean-style buildings. It's a unique African city, like nowhere else I've ever seen.

On one of the days, I met some children who were on their way to school. I stopped and said hello to them. Even though I couldn't speak fluent Portuguese, I communicated with them using signs and the few phrases I had learnt. The children were happy children, I even took some pictures with them.

Maputo, Mozambique

In Maputo, I did all my sightseeing on foot. There were so many buildings that caught my attention. A steel and glass hotel – which is was shaped like two eggs, caught my attention. Another was San Antonio da Polana Church near Avenida Kwame Nkrumah. The church is shaped like a trapezium and looks like a 'lemon squeezer'. That's what the locals call it. San Antonio da Polana church is different. The shape of its roof reminded me of Sydney Opera House.

San Antonio da Polana Church – Maputo, Mozambique

Another thing that I liked about Maputo was the way the street names commemorated Africans or African countries. These included Kwame Nkrumah, Kenneth Kaunda, Sekou Toure, Samora Machel; or Avenida de Zimbabwe. In the city centre, I admired the Central Bank of Mozambique building, all steel and glass, with a stylish orange car park.

I was very happy to see a new bridge being constructed, the Maputo-Catembe bridge. When it is completed, it will connect Maputo to a town called Catembe, which is on the other side of the river. It will be the longest suspension bridge in Africa. I can't wait to see how beautiful it will look when it's finished.

One thing I didn't like about Maputo was that some parts of the city was very dirty. I am always unhappy to see rubbish heaped on the streets and plastic bags flying all over the place. Because Mozambique is rich in natural resources – fertile soils, natural gas, bauxite, coal, graphite and has abundant natural beauty – a beautiful coastline, wildlife, flora and fauna, it could become a wealthy country and its economy could grow if all its natural resources are used well. Maputo made a big impression on me, one I didn't expect.

Chapter Twelve

Beautiful Mbabane

From Maputo, I went to The Kingdom of Swaziland. I get excited whenever I have to travel by road; away from a city or capital. From Maputo, we went past towns like Matola, and Boane. Since I was given a hard time entering Mozambique at the Machipanda border, I prayed that coming back into Mozambique would be easy. In Mhlumeni, on the Swazi side of the border, it was smooth. I was impressed with the immigration staff, how they handled customers. I even liked their uniform.

Once we crossed the border into Swaziland, we drove for about an hour and arrived in Manzini, and from there I jumped on another vehicle to take me to the capital, Mbabane (pronounced Mbabanee). Mbabane is green and lush, and surrounded by the Mdimba mountains. The Matsapha-Mbanane-Ngwenya highway is constructed through the valley, on top of the hills and around the hills. When you are on that road, you get stunning views of Mbabane.

I walked around the city, visited a local market and sampled a local dish; *pap, greens*, and *beef*. The greens were very bitter, like '*shiwaca*' in Ghana or '*bitter leaf*' in Nigeria. If you haven't eaten this before, you will complain about its bitterness. I had eaten bitter leaves many times so it didn't feel that bitter to me.

Swaziland was a pleasant surprise. Most of the stories I'd heard about Swaziland were quite negative but when I got there, I realised there were plenty of positive things about the country, too. For example, most people in Swaziland are paid much more than most people in Ghana, Kenya and Nigeria. Swaziland is a small country, both in land area, and population. It has a population of over 1.4 million people. The 'Swazi Lilangeni' is the currency here, I'd never seen it before. The South African Rand is also legal tender here.

I spent only a day in Swaziland and then went back to Maputo. Immediately I arrived in Maputo, I went home, had a quick shower, had something to eat and I was on my way out again, back to Chimoio.

Immediately the bus left the stand at 2am, I went to sleep. Because I was familiar with the route, I didn't feel that tired. The journey was bearable. After we had been on the road for 10 hours, I got the feeling we were not going to arrive on time because the bus was crawling. When we got to Save, an internal border town, I saw our driver give money to the policeman; he bribed him. This meant we didn't have to get off the bus and cross the border. The bus simply drove through.

No immigration officer even asked me for a bribe on this trip, which has sometimes happened before. We arrived at Inchope just after 9pm. It was only another hour to Chimoio, but our driver decided he was wasn't going any further, and we'd have to spend the night there. When I asked him why, he said it was dangerous to travel at night. I didn't believe that story because other vehicles were heading to Chimoio. Another passenger told me the truth – the driver wanted to pick up more passengers at 4am the next morning, and that was why he didn't want to continue the journey. Some passengers took their bags and left. I took mine and left with two other women. It was very late at night now so I couldn't get a minibus, the only way I could get to Chimoio was get on a long haulage truck. Get on a haulage truck? That wasn't something I was very keen to do.

The trucks were passing by quickly but I was hesitant to join one. After a while, a driver walked past me, so I asked him if he was going my way. He said yes and that I could join him. He told me how much he would charge, and I agreed to his fare. He asked me to sit in the front of the truck and asked the others – five men – to sit on the trailer. There was no space inside the truck so they had to sit outside. They were also carrying a goat. The weather was cold and I was concerned about the men sitting on the open trailer. The driver assured me that they would be fine, and that he picked up passengers on a daily basis. The road was perfectly safe, nothing like our bus driver had suggested. There were many other haulage trucks on the road.

An hour and half later, we arrived in Chimoio. I got a taxi to take me to my hostel, but before I could jump in the vehicle, four policemen surrounded me and asked me to produce my passport. They then searched my luggage. When they realised I wasn't a smuggler or anyone sinister, they tried to delay me and see if I would give them any money. I was patient, and with no chance of extracting money from me, they let me go.

I was thrilled to have finally arrived in Chimoio, twenty-two-and-a-half hours after I set off in Maputo. I took a shower and went straight to bed.

At midday the following day, I was off again, back to Zimbabwe.

Chapter Thirteen
Run an Elephant is Coming

I crossed the border into Zimbabwe and caught a bus to Bulawayo. Though I was exhausted, I couldn't sleep because the bus kept stopping every few kilometres. At every stop, passengers got off and more passengers would board. We stopped at Mvuma for a twenty-minute break, then Gweru, arriving at Bulawayo at 2am the next day. Most of the passengers alighted, then the driver parked the bus in a safe spot and the rest of us slept till daybreak. In the morning, I got a taxi and headed for another bus station in town. I was going all the way to Victoria Falls in the Western region of Zimbabwe.

Once we set off, I noticed how sparsely populated that part of Zimbabwe is. When we arrived in Victoria Falls, I was overjoyed. Over twenty-four hours since I'd set off, here I was, I had made it safely. Exhausted, I jumped in a taxi and headed for Mambo Backpackers village, where I was staying.

I took that much needed shower, had a delicious bowl of *sadza* and *beef sauce*, and went to bed really early.

I woke up to the thrumming sound of helicopters. The Falls were within walking distance from where I was staying, so one could hear the tourist helicopters. I decided to walk to the Falls to get a feel of the town. A small town with 33,000 inhabitants, Victoria Falls town is green, orderly and much cleaner than Harare or the other parts of Zimbabwe I had seen. Apart from those who work for government agencies, hospitals, and a few other sectors, most residents are involved in tourism; hotels, tour companies etc.

Livingstone Way, the road leading to the Falls, was beautiful, with lots of restaurants, shops, and hotels. I turned off Livingstone Way, onto a path leading to the Falls. That's when I met Prio and Advance, two Zimbabweans who worked around the Falls.

I felt a sudden and forceful shove as Prio grabbed my arm and pushed me forward. I wondered what was happening, and he shouted, 'Look! An elephant!'

I couldn't believe it. The elephant was massive and was walking towards us. We both ran like Usain Bolt. Advance ran backwards also to safety. About fifteen seconds later, we stopped running because we were out of the elephant's sight. I was shaking like a leaf. How on earth could this happen? The guys saw how frightened I was, and started laughing at me. They told me they see elephants almost daily on that path. I couldn't believe what I was hearing. I wondered why there was no sign on the road indicating that this is an 'Elephant Zone so beware'. The area we were walking is the Victoria Falls National Park where African elephants, buffalo, and white rhinoceros can be seen.

I thanked God for escaping from the elephant. It took me a while to get over the elephant incident. Advance and Prio had a shop near the Falls, they sold art work and rented raincoats. You need a raincoat if you're going anywhere near the Falls, so I rented one from Advance and made my way to the entrance.

Chapter Fourteen
Thundering Victoria Falls

Victoria Falls is known in the Tonga language as Mosi-ao-Tunya; 'The Smoke That Thunders'. It is considered to be the largest waterfalls in the world, based on the sheet of falling water. Just to give you an idea how massive it is – it's twice the size of Niagara Falls. You can only attempt to compare Iguazu Falls in Argentina and Brazil to Victoria Falls. No other waterfall is as immense.

The water from the Falls is so forceful that before I even got inside the Falls area, I could feel its spray, like rain drizzling on me. I saw Livingstone's statue. It is believed that David Livingstone was the first European to see the Falls. He was a Scottish missionary and explorer. He travelled through Southern and Central Africa preaching to the Chiefs and locals. During his day, slaves were bought and sold. He wanted to end the African slave trade.

I could see the Falls in the distance. The further I walked down the trail, the more I saw how gigantic they were. When I got to Viewpoint 6, close to the main falls, the roar of the water was unbelievable. I also started to get wet. As I got closer and closer, I saw it in all its glory. The Falls are massive, gigantic, and majestic. I was in awe. I just stood there staring at this natural wonder. Though I was getting wetter and wetter, I didn't move. I was completely blown away.

Then I moved further and I saw the rainbow which always appears. Brightly lit in the background, it was clear and showing all the colours. By this time, I was soaked. The raincoat I was wearing couldn't protect me from the gush of the water. I found a sunny spot and while I waited for my clothes to dry, I continued to admire this unique waterfall. Victoria Falls had touched my heart and I didn't want to leave. I just wanted to camp there for a few days until I was satisfied.

The largest waterfalls in the world – Victoria Falls, Zimbabwe

The whole evening, my mind and heart was on the Falls. Victoria Falls had truly been one of the most spectacular sights I had ever seen. I was completely overwhelmed. Because I was thinking about the falls so much, I had a feeling I would even dream about it.

I left Victoria Falls town the next day and crossed into Zambia.

When I crossed into Zambia, I saw monkeys jumping all over the place. These monkeys in the National Park often come out to search for food. I was told that if you have food in your hand, they will jump on you and collect the food from your hand. When I heard this, I immediately hid the food I was holding in my bag.

I boarded a taxi to Livingstone, a city in the Southern Province of Zambia. In Livingstone, I visited the museum and learned about the history of the country.

Next, I headed to the bus station to get a bus to Lusaka, the capital. It's a long way. On the road, I saw beautiful and unique trees. Trees I had never seen before. I admired Zambia's natural vegetation.

We arrived in Lusaka at 8:30pm. I was staying with my dear friends, Lucy and her husband Frank. I knew they would feed me and look after me. I was very happy to see them. We talked till we were dropping off to sleep.

On Sunday, I joined Lucy and Frank at the church they attend, the Miracle Life Family Church. The church was beautiful and organized. I had a great time listening to Pastor Walker. For lunch, Lucy and Frank gave me a treat at Taj Pamodzi Hotel, where I ate till I almost needed a caterpillar to move me from my chair. I told them that had I known we were having lunch at the Taj, I would have fasted for forty days and forty nights.

I spent several days indoors, eating, sleeping and writing. I was so tired from all the long bumpy bus rides I had taken. Some parts of Lusaka looked like some parts of Accra. I visited Embassy Park —where three former presidents of Zambia are buried. Like most African countries, Zambia has enormous potential. It should be a rich country because of the vast amounts of copper, uranium, fertile land, and human resources. But it hasn't yet achieved its potential.

When it was time to leave Lusaka, I was sad. I didn't want to go. I'd had such an enjoyable and restful time that a part of me wanted to stay. But I was going to Ethiopia, a country I looked forward to visiting. I said goodbye to Zambia, goodbye to Lucy and her loving family and embraced what lay ahead.

Chapter Fifteen

Coffee Country

Ethiopia was my seventy-second country overall and fifth country on this trip. When I got out of the airport, Yared, the son my host, had a taxi waiting to pick me. We jumped in and headed for their home in Kazanchis, an area in Addis Ababa. I was staying with Mma Gennet, Yared's mother. We spent some time chatting before I went to bed. I'd chosen to stay with Mma Gennet and her family because I wanted to experience Ethiopian culture.

The next morning, I went to the Djibouti embassy. Djibouti was the next country on my list and I needed a visa. Unfortunately, I didn't get it because I needed to provide further documents. I had to return another day.

I spent the afternoon walking around Addis Ababa. Addis Ababa is a city under construction. There were many, many buildings being built. In one area alone, I counted about fifty construction sites. Ethiopia is growing, and needs more roads, houses, hotels and offices. It really is opening up for business.

For lunch and dinner, I ate *injera*, the traditional Ethiopian dish, made with a cereal called teff. Teff is similar to wheat. Though I didn't like it very much because it's sour, I knew I'd have to get used to eating it because at the local restaurants I went to, *Injera* was the only option available.

That evening, I witnessed an Ethiopian tradition – a coffee ceremony. Mma Gennet invited some friends over for this ceremony. She cut fresh green grass and sprinkled it on the floor of her living room. She then made a big pot of freshly brewed coffee for us to drink. The rich dark colour and aroma of the coffee was inviting. The coffee was tasty too. Ethiopia is where coffee beans were first seen or tasted. It's the fifth-largest exporter of coffee in the world, and a large amount of the money it makes come from coffee.

Coffee Ceremony – Addis Ababa, Ethiopia

The next morning, I got a bus to Woldia, a town in the Northern Region of Ethiopia. From there, I was going to Laibela. I'd been told the journey would take two days.

When we got out of Addis Ababa, the scenery really changed. To my left and to my right were beautiful mountains stretching as far as the eye could see. We stopped to have lunch, in a town called Kemise, and I wanted to eat something different. I tried communicating this to the waiter, but after two orders, he still brought me *injera*. I was frustrated and upset because I was hungry and our bus was leaving. Another customer who saw our sign language from afar came to my rescue. Thankfully he could speak a little bit of English, and helped me order what I wanted.

Ethiopia is the second largest country in Africa by population. It's also the most populous landlocked country in the world. It has a population of about 100 million people. It's one of the two countries in Africa that was never colonised (Liberia is the other). It was only briefly occupied by the Italians from 1936-1941. Since it was never colonised, by either the French, English, Spanish, or Portuguese, its language never changed. It's original language, Amharic, is the official language. This makes talking with locals very difficult. Most locals don't speak a word of English. Before coming here, I had never heard a word of Amharic, but now here I was, hearing it every day and learning how to speak it – the basics, anyway, like 'good morning' and 'thank you'.

Here are some phrases I learnt in Amharic:

እንደምን አደራችሁ (indemin aderatschu) – *Good morning*

ሰላም ጤና ይስጥልኝ (selam tena jistilign) – *Hello*

አመሰግናለው (ameseginalew) – *Thank you*

አማርኛ አላናገርም (amarigna alinagerim) – *I don't speak any Ahmaric*

እንግሊዘኛ (inglisegna) – *English*

የመጣሁት ከ ... ነው። (jemetahut ke ... new) – *I'm from*

On the way to Woldia, we went through Kombolcha. Here a brand-new railway is being built, the Awash-Kombolcha-Hara Gebaya Railway. It's being constructed by a Turkish construction company. When the railway is opened, it will ease traffic and service the people of Ethiopia. After Dessie, another city on our way, the landscape became even more dramatic, and much more beautiful.

Ethiopian Mountains

Ethiopia is a high-altitude country – this means that a lot of towns and cities are located 2,000m above sea level. Once you are in the mountains, the colours in the valleys are yellow, green, and black. Colours of teff and the rich black soil. Looking down into the valleys, the views were extremely beautiful. I thoroughly enjoyed travelling by road, even though the roads were often narrow and winding. There were no barriers at the edges of the road, so sometimes when an oncoming vehicle was approaching you could be a little frightened.

When we arrived in Woldia, I tried getting another vehicle to Lalibela, but it was too late in the day. Because the roads were steep and dangerous, people didn't travel at night. I found myself a room in a hotel nearby and checked in. At dinner time, I was happy to be eating rice. I spoke some little Amharic and used sign language to let the receptionist know what I wanted to eat and it worked! I ate the rice while smiling. I was very happy.

Chapter Sixteen
Miracle Churches

I woke up the next morning smelling of urine. I wondered why – for a second I thought maybe I'd accidentally urinated on the bed. I touched my skirt and it was dry. That's when I realised the bed I slept in was urine infested. I quickly washed my clothes, took a cold shower, and got ready for my long day ahead.

I got a ride with an Ethiopian family who were also staying in the hotel. They were going to Lalibela, so I joined them and we set off very early.

The nice view of the mountains continued, on either side of the road. The mountains were even more dramatic and were unusually formed. Some portions of the road were also more dangerous; untarred, narrower, and high. After five hours, when we arrived in a town before Lalibela, I had to get off, and found a tuk-tuk to take me the rest of the way. I couldn't relax for the whole thirty minutes I was on the tuk-tuk because the road was so narrow. It was a scary experience, a pure adventure.

In Lalibela, I was met by a friend of my host, Meles, who took me to where I was staying. Once I'd put my bag down and had something to eat – *injera* again – I headed for the rock-hewn churches, my main reason for coming to Lalibela. These churches are world-famous, and were cut from the 'living rock' – which means they weren't built from bricks or quarried stone, but carved directly from the rock. They are probably Ethiopia's most famous buildings and tourists travel from far away to see them.

I visited the largest church on the site, House of the Saviour of the World. Seeing how large it was, I couldn't believe how such a huge structure could be cut out of a rock. What tools did the builders use? How exactly did they cut the rock until it formed into this? I kept asking myself.

On the day I went, they were celebrating the feast of Saint Michael so there were many locals in the churches to worship. They came in their traditional clothing. I then went to St Michael's church, the most spectacular of all the churches.

Lalibela, Ethiopia

The Largest Rock Church – Lalibela, Ethiopia

St Michael's Church – Lalibela, Ethiopia

St Michael's Church – Lalibela, Ethiopia

Looking at the churches, it was hard to believe humans built them. Some locals actually believe that whiles humans worked in the day to build the churches, angels helped them at night. I was reminded again of how gifted and creative humans are. I really enjoyed seeing the churches. For dinner, I was happy to be eating rice. My time in Lalibela was short but well spent. The next day I had to go back to Addis Ababa and this time around I was even keener to make the trip in a day, and not two days. I hoped my plan would work.

I got on a local bus to Dessie, one that was much cheaper and very basic. It stopped at almost every village to pick passengers up and drop some off. Thankfully we made it to Dessie around 3pm and I found another vehicle going to Addis Ababa. I was very happy. It was a minibus, and not a very comfortable one, but I was glad to be moving on. Once I was back in Addis Ababa, I'd be able to follow up on my visa to Djibouti. It was a long drive back. The roads were pitch dark and winding. Just before midnight, we arrived safely in Addis Ababa. I did a dance in my head because I was too tired to do so physically. I was so thankful to God for bringing me back safely.

Because of the distance I'd covered in the last few days, I was exhausted. I felt sick, and wondered if I would have the strength to go to Djibouti. I knew going to Djibouti by road would be a real challenge. I prayed, asking God for supernatural strength and decided to sleep to see how I felt in the morning.

My prayers were answered – I woke up energised and ready for anything. I went to the Djibouti Embassy, and this time, I picked up my visa.

Once I'd collected the visa, I bought my ticket from the Selam bus station at Meskel Square. Addis Ababa has a light rail train. This train is the first of its kind in Sub-Saharan Africa. It was opened in 2015. Because of this light railway, so many people in Addis Ababa can get to work and to school on time.

Light Railway – Addis Ababa, Ethiopia

Chapter Seventeen

Tuk-tuks, Djibouti & My Crazy Friend Francis

The next day, I went to the bus station very early in the morning to get a bus to Dire Dawa, a city in the eastern region of Ethiopia. Once we got out of Addis Ababa, we got on a brand new expressway; the Addis Ababa – Adama Express Highway. It is an 85km six-lane highway. This expressway is the first of its kind in Ethiopia. When I saw it, I exclaimed; Wow! I was impressed with it. I really enjoyed the one-hour drive on this road and wished that Ghana had such an expressway – currently we don't.

On the way, I saw another railway being constructed. It is the Addis Ababa-Djibouti railway line. We arrived in Dire Dawa late afternoon. I found the station for the buses leaving for the Djibouti border and bought the ticket for the next part of my journey.

Dire Dawa was hot, dry, and the market area bustling. There are tuk-tuks all over the city. Tuktuks are the main means of transport. I was even surprised and happy to see some female drivers of the tuktuks. Until now, I had never seen a woman driving one.

My bus to Dewele on the border of Ethiopia was a night bus, so I found a cheap hotel to take a shower and rest in before the bus departed. At 7pm I made my way back to the bus garage. When I got there, there were a number of passengers waiting. Some men were seated on a cardboard or mat with their legs stretched out chewing khat, smoking, drinking Coke and chatting.

Khat is the leaves of a tree, traditionally consumed in Ethiopia, Djibouti, Somalia, Kenya and Yemen. Khat makes you feel high. It is classified as a drug of abuse by the World Health Organization. In other parts of the world, if you are found selling or buying khat, you will be punished. But here in Ethiopia, khat is freely chewed.

When I saw the driver was also chewing khat, I became worried. Travelling by road at night was already something I didn't want to do because the roads are narrow. Wondering if I should go ahead or not, I realised this was the only way to Djibouti if I wanted to go by public transport. If I really wanted to go to Djibouti by road, I had no choice, it was this bus or nothing. Around 9pm, boarding started. It was a dog-eat-dog kind of boarding. The passengers and conductor were shouting, shoving, and pushing. The bus was crammed, some passengers sat on gallons in the middle of the bus. When I got on, I was shouted at to put my bags away. Surprised at how the conductor spoke to me, I quizzed him, then he shouted even louder. This was creating a scene, so I told him I was getting off the bus. With his hands, he asked me to get off, speaking Ahmaric. He then screamed at me some more. I felt quite sad.

Fortunately, his supervisor could speak a bit of English so I narrated the incident to him. I was then given another ticket for the next bus. I was relieved to be away from the drama. The next bus arrived before 11pm, but when I saw it, I wondered if I'd made the right decision to get off the first one. This second bus was pure metal with wheels. This bus was a former truck which had been converted and fitted with seats, it looked like it would break down soon. Travelling at night along those narrow roads and experiencing a breakdown, would certainly not be fun. All I could do was pray. God himself had to steer this 'metal' to our destination.

The police checkpoints on the way were uncountable. Every so often we had to get down and show our passports. Even though I was sleepy, I struggled to get any rest. The bumpy road, uncomfortable seat and frequent stops prevented me. At 6:30am we got to the border in Dewele. I was thankful to have finally arrived.

I stamped my passport and jumped on another vehicle heading to Djibouti City. At the Djiboutian border in Gelille, officials were fascinated by my story. They couldn't understand why I was travelling by road all alone.

I just explained to them that I was a crazy African Woman visiting every country in the world and that Djibouti was my seventy-third country. Another topic of conversation generated by my passport was football. Once they saw the passport they excitedly started talking about football, mentioning players like Asamoah Gyan, and the Ayew brothers. I couldn't believe how far football was carrying us. I didn't just get these comments here, but through every African country I'd visited. Football was putting Ghana on the map, or rather the lips of other Africans.

After our bags were searched, we got on the bus and went on our way. Once we were on Djiboutian soil, I started to notice how hot the country was. It was 40 degrees Celsius. The weather was humid too. I felt uncomfortable. Thankfully the road was tarred, and in two and a half hours we arrived in Djibouti City. I was relieved.

I was sweating profusely, and made my way to African Village, the hotel where I was staying. Even though it was the cheapest hotel I could find in the city, it was expensive. I paid more here than I paid in Switzerland, Norway, or Singapore.

Because of the heat, I was tempted to stay indoors. But I resisted the temptation and went out to see the city. Djibouti, a country in the Horn of Africa, occupies a small land area and has a population of about 850,000 citizens. A former French colony, it gained independence in 1977. Djibouti is famous for its salt, it has the world's largest salt reserve in Lake Assal. Salt is an area the government is trying to exploit – just a few days before I arrived, the government commissioned a port, just for salt export. The government of Djibouti wants to cash in on its white gold.

Because it was Ramadan, the streets were virtually empty. Most shops were closed and the residents indoors. I discovered that in the daytime during Ramadan, shops are closed, and most people don't go to work. Though I like to eat local food sold along the street, I couldn't find a single vendor open for business.

A Traditional Hut – Djibouti City, Djibouti

Djibouti is one of the least visited countries in the world, not many tourists come here. It was my last country on this six-country tour so I had to head back to Ethiopia the next day. By this time, I was tired and looking forward to going home to Ghana. Having something to eat at the hotel, I met another African, a Zimbabwean. Since I had travelled extensively through Zimbabwe, we struck up a conversation. Levison, now working in Yemen, was on his way to Harare. Meeting him, I was reminded again of how many Zimbabweans are now living and working far from their country.

The next day, I decided to leave, and start the challenging journey back. Because Djibouti is not frequently visited, particularly by road, it was hard to find any information about buses going to Ethiopia. I got to the bus station only to be informed it was a night bus. I was wondering what to do in the sweltering heat, when a local, who saw how lost I was, came to my rescue. He offered to take me to the police station to wait there. Fortunately, it was close by. When we arrived, Mohammed the officer gave me a comfortable place to sit. His office had a fan so I was away from the heat. I told him I was hungry and needed to buy food, he went out and got me cakes, drinks and water. I couldn't believe his generosity. He kept telling me I was his guest. I was thankful to him for helping me.

I sat there for nearly eight hours then headed back to the station. This time, the bus was waiting. As it was night and the fast was over, vendors were all over the street selling food. Since I'd hardly eaten all day, I was very hungry. I ate all the food I bought in no time.

The city centre really came to life when people had broken their fast. Shops were opening and there were cars on the streets. Even though it was night, it was still very hot and humid with temperatures above 35 degrees Celsius. The smell from my body and clothes was so bad I wanted to cut off my nose. The weather was something else.

At 9:30pm, we left Djibouti City, arriving at the border at midnight. The border was closed, and we had to wait till it opened in the morning. Some locals rented out mattresses and mats for passengers to sleep on. A fellow passenger, Idel, a young Djiboutian/Ethiopian who took a liking to me (obviously realising I was a stranger and needed help) became my interpreter. I rented a mat to sleep on. The mosquitoes, like houseflies were buzzing around my ears. I kept hitting my body in an attempt to drive the mosquitoes away. I couldn't sleep. A local saw I was struggling to sleep and gave me his mosquito net to sleep in. I was super grateful. Now I could sleep.

Sleeping at the border – Djibouti

I slept like a baby and woke up around 6am when our vehicle was due to leave. After I crossed, I rented a wheelbarrow and a porter, who pushed my bags to Dewele, on the Ethiopian side.

I was over the moon once I got into Ethiopia and boarded a vehicle back to Dire Dawa. I knew the most difficult part of my journey was over. Though I still had seven hours of travel ahead of me, I was light hearted. I couldn't wait to arrive in Dire Dawa and take a shower because the stench from my body and clothes was so much worse now.

The drive back felt long and exhausting. By midday, I had had enough and kept looking at the map to see how far we had left to travel. The joy I felt when we zoomed into Dire Dawa was uncontrollable but I was too tired to celebrate. When I got back to Genery hotel, I was tempted to throw away my clothes and my trainers. But I didn't throw them away because I loved those clothes and trainers very much. I quickly washed them and took a long, long, shower. The dirt washing from my body was like a light cup of coffee or Milo. Being under the shower felt like heaven.

Starving, I made some instant noodles and ate, and later went roaming the streets of Dire Dawa. As I was exhausted, I went early to bed.

I woke up bright and early, and headed for the bus station. I was making my way back to Addis Ababa. I was thrilled to be heading back not only because my trip was over but also because I was meeting Francis Tapon, my friend and fellow adventurer. Francis, the crazy guy I travelled in Namibia with, was ending his trip in Africa. He had been on the continent for the last five years and had seen fifty countries, with only four more to go.

When we met then, he was single, but now he is married to Rejoice, a Cameroonian, and they were travelling the world together. We chatted and chatted, comparing notes, and sharing stories. We had both seen and experienced more of the world. I had now been to seventy-three countries, and he, one hundred and eleven countries. Our understanding about the world and especially about the countries in Africa was much deeper and broader.

We both agreed about the positive things we had seen and experienced on the continent. Some of those positive things are our hospitable nature, our patience, and our level of optimism. We also talked about the negative things we had seen; like, not being curious or not asking questions. Asking questions is very important – it makes you a better informed person.

I said goodbye to Francis and Rejoice, and promised to see them again. Who knows, next time we may meet in Uzbekistan in Central Asia.

On the morning I was flying back to Accra, I was so excited. I was thankful to God for protecting me and for helping me on this trip. The four-and-a-half-hour flight went by quickly because I was writing and thinking about all that I had experienced in the last five weeks.

I had covered 24,426km, nearly half of that was by road. I had eaten unusual foods, slept in strange beds, ridden in metal vehicles called 'buses', met kind people, and visited beautiful sites. I had learnt a lot and had been challenged, I'd laughed, and at times wanted to cry. I had grown up and had been shown so much kindness. But most especially, I had so much fun travelling. I will do this over, and over, and over, and over, and over again because the countries I visited are indeed beautiful.

I will continue to see the world, one country at a time.

Though I have seen thirty-one countries in Africa and still have twenty-three more to go, I will give Africa a break. I will possibly travel through Africa again in five years. I haven't been to South America, it's a continent I want to see next!!!!

APPENDICES

DISTANCES TRAVELLED FROM MY MOST RECENT TRIP TO SOUTHERN & EAST AFRICA

Date	From	To	Distance	M. of Travel	Duration
24/05/2017	Accra, Ghana	Addis Ababa, Ethiopia	4,320km	Air	5:40hrs
24/05/2017	Addis Ababa, Ethiopia	Lusaka, Zambia	2,940km	Air	4hrs
25/05/2017	Lusaka, Zambia	Harare, Zimbabwe	495km	Road	10:30hrs
30/05/2017	Harare, Zimbabwe	Chimoio, Mozambique	360km	Road	8hrs
31/05/2017	Chimoio, Mozambique	Maputo, Mozambique	1,140km	Road	19:30hrs
05/06/2017	Maputo, Mozambique	Mbabane, Swaziland	228km	Road	4hrs
05/06/2017	Mbabane, Swaziland	Maputo, Mozambique	228km	Road	5:30
06/06/2017	Maputo, Mozambique	Chimoio, Mozambique	1,140km	Road	23 hrs
07/06/2017	Chimoio, Mozambique	Mutare, Zimbabwe	97km	Road	2hrs
07/06/2017	Mutare, Zimbabwe	Bulawayo, Zimbabwe	561km	Road	8hrs
08/06/2017	Bulawayo, Zimbabwe	Victoria Falls, Zimbabwe	441km	Road	7hrs
10/06/2017	Victoria Falls, Zimbabwe	Livingstone, Zambia	12.2km	Road	1hr
10/06/2017	Livingstone, Zambia	Lusaka, Zambia	483km	Road	7hrs

15/06/2017	Lusaka, Zambia	Addis Ababa, Ethiopia	3,740km	Air, via Harare	7:30hrs
17/06/2017	Addis Ababa, Ethiopia	Woldia, Ethiopia	506km	Road	10:30hrs
18/06/2017	Woldia, Ethiopia	Lalibela, Ethiopia	180km	Road	5hrs
19/06/2017	Lalibela, Ethiopia	Dessie, Ethiopia	298km	Road	9:30hrs
19/06/2017	Dessie, Ethiopia	Addis Ababa, Ethiopia	387km	Road	10hrs
21/06/2017	Addis Ababa, Ethiopia	Dire Dawa, Ethiopia	445km	Road	9:30hrs
22/06/2017	Dire Dawa, Ethiopia	Dewele, Ethiopia	215km	Road	7hrs
23/06/2017	Dewele, Ethiopia	Djibouti City, Djibouti	115km	Road	3hrs
24/06/2017	Djibouti City, Djibouti	Dewele, Ethiopia	115km	Road	3hrs
24/06/2017	Dewele, Ethiopia	Dire Dawa, Ethiopia	215km	Road	7 hours
25/06/2017	Dire Dawa, Ethiopia	Addis Ababa, Ethiopia	445km	Road	9:30 hrs
26/06/2017	Addis Ababa, Ethiopia	Accra, Ghana	4,320km	Air	4:10hrs

TOTAL KILOMETERS TRAVELLED IN 5 WEEKS - 24,426km

About the Author

Princess Umul Hatiyya Ibrahim Mahama is an Adventurer, Writer, Teacher, and Entrepreneur. Her mission in life is to inspire others to live their lives to the full. Princess has embarked on adventures all over the world. Some of the crazy things she has done are:

- Cycling from Accra – Tamale in Ghana to raise funds to build a school
- Climbing Mountain Afadjato in Ghana
- Climbing Table Mountain in South Africa
- Bungy Jumping in New Zealand

Princess is currently visiting every country in the world. Some of the countries she has been to are Australia, Bosnia & Hercegovina, Canada, Ethiopia, Iceland, Japan, and Zimbabwe. Princess has been interviewed on radio, TV and various online platforms in Ghana, Nigeria, Malawi as well as on the BBC. She is married to Michael Apreko and they are parents of six girls. When she is not on the road, she can be found in Accra, Ghana.

Princess shares her travel stories at

www.theglobetrottingprincess.com